The Shaping

Book 1
Satan's Saga

A modern English rendering
of the Ælfrædian English
Genesis Poem(s)
by
Douglas Ryan VanBenthuysen
aka
Parch

(The Image "Abel's Tree" on page 65
provided by Frida Portugal at the
intersection of 6th & Trinity in
Austin, Texas)

Published by
Words by Parch, Austin, TX
July 2018

The Shaping, Book 1:
Satan's Saga

Published by Words by Parch
Austin, Texas, USA
July 2018

ISBN: 0692148906
ISBN-13: 978-0692148907

Introduction

Oh Pius One, if I could another advise,
Bearing in mind what I have already said
                    concerning blank verse,
I would only say: keep your line alive.
THUS END DISCLAIMER
            ...ten lines left...must be terse.

I have heard from he who hails from the
Pacific Northwest. He claimed Anemic Royalty.
Some say he shot his face off with a
Shotgun. But his girl be as cute as a bean.

You seek to cut your line, but much
                    more slowly.
With whom do you suppose the Beatrice
                    will fly?

It ain't me! Nor Milton! 'Tis you, Louisely
Intellected one! I pripee: Multiply.

A garden's lost when farmers fail to seed it,
Or leave unplucked; perchance a fool may
                    weed it.

The Medium is The Message

Marshall McLuhan

THE SHAPING

I. Satan's Saga

.i. The Love-Song and the Fall

For us, it is right—very much so—that we praise the skies' guard, the riders' wonder-king, with words, that we love with our moods. He is the craftiest, the head of all, the high creatures' almighty lord. Before him came no cause, before him came no origin, nor will the eternal chieftain's end come now, but he will always be an elder with high power over heaven's seats.

Truth-fast and strength-holding, he held the skies' bosoms, which had been set wide and far through god's welding for wonder's sons, for the ghosts' guards. They had splendor and joy, and the troops of angels had their first-source's bright bliss.

Their fame was great!

The glorious thanes praised their prince, sang his love lustily. They worshiped their

With the chieftain's goods, they were quite
blessed. They knew nothing of sins, the doing
of crimes, but they lived in eternal peace
with their elder. They didn't begin to raise
anything else in the skies except the right
and the true, until when a faction of the
angels became lost in error out of over-
mindfulness. They no longer willed to act
to their own benefit, but they turned from
god's kin-love. They had a great boast that
they had the power to break-up the wondrous
house, wide and sky-bright, with an army's
force against the chieftain.

There, sorrow, envy, and over-mindfulness
befell them and that angel's mood, he who
first began working, weaving, and wreaking
ill-array. Then he spoke with a word, thirsting
for evil, that he willed to own a home and
high-seat in the north part of heavens' kingdom
Then god became irate and wrathful with

with the riders whom he honored before with
light and wonder. For the oath-breakers, he
shaped a wretched home, hell-sounds, hard-curses,
with work as a reward. Our chieftain ordered
ghosts' guards to bide the exiles' pain-house,
deep and joyless. Then he knew it readily: covered
by endless night, filled with misery, folded
around with fire and great cold, smoke and
red flame. Then he ordered waxing penal
terrors.

They had heaped up a grim series of wrongs
against god

For that, a grim reward befell them.

The wrathful beings said they willed to
own the kingdom and they easily might just
so. This belief failed them since the wielder,
the heavens' high king, raised his hand
highest against that army. The mindless may
not share might, mean against the meter,
but the famous one split their mood, debased
pride.

Then he became enraged. He slew the sin-scathers with victory and power, with doom and glory, and he cut his enemies off from joy, protection, and all safety, and bright fame, and he wreaked his anger swiftly on his foes though his own might with the strongest casting-down. It had grimly enraged his stern mood. He gripped in wrath, with hostile hands, and broke them in an embrace, irate in mood. He drove those who strove against him from the homeland, the wonder-homestead.

Then our creator thrust and cut the over-proud angels' race, the oathless army, from heaven. The wielder sent the loathsome-minded militia, gloomy ghosts, on a long trek. For them, the vow was forfeit, the boast humbled, and the glory debased, the light stained. Ever since, they have hovered in exile, in the dark; they had no need to laugh loudly, but they dwelled wearily with hell-torment and knew woe, pain and sorrow. They suffered misery, thatched with shadow, a severe after-reward, that which they had begun to win against God.

Then it was, as formerly, truth; peace in heaven, fair protection customs, lord loved by all, the prince by his thanes. The loyal ones', the joy-havers', glory waxed with the chieftain.

.ii. The Stern-Souled King Shapes Middle-Earth

They were united, those who live in the sky, wonders' native land. Enmity did not spring up, doom or cursed war among the angels, since the rebel militia, bereft of light, gave up heaven. Seats, rich and wide, stood in their tracks with wonderous genitive power, growing with gifts in god's kingdom, bright and glory-fast, ownerless since the weary ghosts went to the exile place, lowly under harmful lock.

Then our prince pondered, in a thoughtful mood, how he might craft the native seats after

he set a better army in the sky-bright hall, those
which the boastful ravagers had given up high in
the heavens. Therefore, holy god reached under the
skies with mighty force. He willed that the earth
and the upper-sky and the wide-water become
set for himself, the crafted world in the wrathfuls'
payment, those whom he sent from protection, the
fallen.

Nothing was here yet, nothing had become
except dark shade, but this wide ground stood
deep and dim, strange to the chieftain, idle
and unused.

The stern-souled king looked with eyes on
that and beheld the place, lacking in joys.
He saw dark mist remaining in endless night,
black under the skies, wan and waste until
the created world came to be through the wonder-
king's word. Here, first, the eternal chieftain,
all creatures' helmet, almighty lord, shaped
heaven and earth, raised up the sky and

established this roomy land with strong might.

The field was yet ungreen with grass. The dark sea thatched wan waves far and wide with black endless night.

The wonder-bright heaven-guard's ghost bore genitive power over the ocean. The angels' meter, life's giver, ordered light to come forth over the roomy ground. The high-king's command was quickly fulfilled. For him, holy light was over the waste as the maker bid.

Then, victories' wielder sundered light against darkness over the sea-flood, shadow against shining. Life's giver shaped names for both. First, through the chieftain's word light was named day, a brightly beautiful creation. Time's bearing forth well pleased the lord at the first day's start. He saw dark, black shadows diminishing the round, broad ground.

-iii- The World is Dealt

Then, the time went, scurrying over middle-earth's timber. The meter, our shaper, shoved the first evening after the shining brightness. Running in its tracks, the gloomy darkness pressed, for which the prince himself shaped the name night.

Our savior sundered them. Ever afterwards, they day and night, continued, and did the chieftain's will, eternally over the earth.

Then, another day came, light after gloominess.. Then life's guard commanded a highest heaven timber to become in the ocean flood's midst. Our welder divided the seas and wrought the skies' vaults. The ruler raised that up from the earth through his own word, lord almighty. The flood was dealt under the high-sky by holy might,

water from the waters, that which
yet remain under the stronghold of
the folks roof.

Then the splendid third morning
came quickly, faring over the fields. For
the meter, there was not yet wide land
nor useful ways, but the field stood
fast, ringed with flood. Through his
words, the angels' lord ordered the
waters, which now hold their run
under the skies, to be together in a
fixed place. Then quickly the ocean
stood together, broad under the heavens,
as the holy one bid.

Then the deep was sundered against
the land. Life's guard, the troops'
herder, saw a widely visible dry place
which the wonder-king named earth.

he set a right run for the waves,
the roomy flood, and fettered...

[HERE, AS SEVERAL PLACES IN THE
JUNIUS MANUSCRIPT, A LEAF IS
MISSING FROM THE MANUSCRIPT)

.iiii. Eve's Creation and Life in Paradise

en the sky's guard, the newly
crafted paradise's herdsman and
protector, did not think it fit
that Adam be alone long. Therefore,
the high king, the lord almighty
made a helper for him, wrought a
wife; and then, life's light-bringer rapidly
gave the beloved warrior a support.

He detached that work from Adam's
body, and skillfully took a rib from
his side. He was resting fast and
softly sleeping. He knew no pain, no
dole of labor. There came not any
blood from the gash, but the angels'
prince took a living bone from the body.

The man was unwounded

From this, god wrought a free female. He put in life, an eternal soul. They were like angels.

Then Adam's bride was given a ghost. They were both light-bright in youth, born in the world by the meter's might. They did not know how to do nor carry out evil, but the chieftain's burning love was in both of their breasts.

Then the bliss-hearted king, all-creation's meter, blessed mankind, the first two, father and mother, wife and warrior.

Then he spoke words: "Now teem and wax, fill the all-green earth with progeny, with your kind, with sons and daughters. Salt water will remain within both of your wielding, and all the world's creation. Enjoy days' fruit and sea's fish and heaven's

birds. Into both of your wielding is given
the holy cattle and the wild beasts and
living things, those which trod the land, the
life abounding kind, those which the flood
wakes around the whale-road all will
obey you two."

Then our shaper gazed upon his works'
light and his glorious new creation's fruit.
Paradise stood good and ghostly, filled with
the future-guarding graces' benefits. The
flowing lake, the welling spring, lit upon
the blissful land. As yet, the clouds, wan
with wind, had not at all born rains
over roomy grounds; however, the fields stood
adorned with fruits.

Out of this new paradise, four noble streams
held their forward runs, which were dealt,
all from one, by the chieftains' might, when

he shaped this earth and sent the light-bright waters into the world. People, the earth-dwellers, human-folk call the one Fison, which surrounds the broad part of the fields outside Hebeleat with bright streams. On this native turf, adventurous men, the tribe's sons from near and far, find gold and gem-kinds, the best ones, those which books tell us about. The second one, whose name is Geon, lies around the land and border guard of Ethiopia's ample kingdom. The third is the Tigris; this over-flowing river lies beside the Assirian tribal border. Likewise is the fourth, which many men among the folk now wise name Euphrates.

[MISSING MANUSCRIPT LEAF]

[OLD SAXON SATAN SECTION BEGINS...]

.V. The Stern-Minded King's Warning

... but you two enjoy all the others for yourselves.
Renounce that one beam, ward yourself against
that fruit. The wills' lack shall not come
to be for you two!

Then they eagerly bowed with heads
toward the heaven king and said thanks
for all, for cunning and this lore. He let
them occupy that land.

Then the holy chiftain, the stern-minded
king, turned himself toward heaven. His
handwork stood together on the sand. They
knew not sorrow as groaning, but they knew
God's will for the longest time. They
were beloved to god while they would
hold his holy word.

.vi. The Rebellion

He all-wielder, holy chieftain, had gathered ten kinds of angels with his hand-power, those whom he trusted that they would follow as his younglings, work his will because he had given them their wits.

And the holy chieftain shaped him with his hands; he had set him so blessedly; he had wrought him so strongly and so mightily in this thoughtful mood. He let him rule so much, highest in the heavens after himself. He had wrought him so brightly; his face, which came to him from the riders' chieftain, was so joyful in the heavens, he was alight like the stars!

He should have worked the chieftain's praise, he should have held dear his

dreaminess in the heavens, and he should
have thanked his chieftain for the reward
he shared with him in the light. Then
he would have let him wield for a long
time. But he wound it into a worse thing
for himself; he began to heave up strife
with heaven's highest wielder, he who
sits on the holy seat.

He was dear to our chieftain. It could
not become hidden from him that his angel
began to be overly moody, heaved himself
up against his master, sought hate-speech
and pride-words.

He would not serve god!

He said that his body was alight and
shiny, white and form-bright. He could not
find in his mind that he would serve God,
the prince, as a youngling. He thought to
himself that he had more might and craft

than the holy God and could have more of
a folk-following.

The overly-moody angel spoke a pile
of words. He thought through his one
craft how he would more strongly wrought
a seat, higher in the heavens. He said
that his mind spurred him on, that
he should begin to work west and north,
strengthening the timber. He said he
thought it doubtful that he would become
God's youngling.

"Why should I work?" he said. "Not a whit
do I need to have a master! I may work
as many of the wonders with my own
hands! I have great ability to wield,
adorning a better seat, higher in heaven.
Why shall I serve for his favor, and bow
to him as such a youngling?

"I can be a god as he is!

"Strong friends, stand by me, you who will not fail me in the strife, hard-mooded helpers. They have chosen me as a master, brave warriors! With such friends, one may think up arrays and, with such a folk-following, carry them out! They are my yearning friends, loyal in their mindshafts.

"I may be their master

"I may array this kingdom.

"So, I think to myself it not right that I need to lower myself a whit before god for anything good. I will no longer be his youngling!"

As he spoke, the all-wielder heard it all, that his angel had begun to heave up great over-mood with his master and dully spoke his words with the chieftain. Then he should pay for that deed, being

dealt the winnings for his work; he
should have his punishment, the most of
all misery

So does each man who begins to strive
with crime against his wielder, against
the famous chieftain.

The mighty one, the heaven's highest
chieftain, became enraged and threw
him off the high seat. He had won
hate from his master, had forfeit his
favor. The good one became grim with
him in his mind. Therefore, he should
seek hard hell, pain's ground, because
he fought with heaven's wielder. Then
he sent him wandering from his favor
and threw him into hell, into the deep
dells, where he became a devil, a fiend
with all his friends

Then they fell from above, out of

heaven, right though three nights and days,
the angels from heaven to hell; and the
chieftain misshaped them all into devils,
because they would not find his deed and
word worthy. He, almighty God, therefore set
them in a worse light in the nether under
the earth, in the dark hell.

There in the long unmet evening, each of
all fiends has renewing fire. Then, on the
dawn, eastern wind comes, fiery cold frost.
Fire or frost, they shall always have some
hard torment. Guilt wrought it for them
as punishment. There world was changed by
the first trek.

Hell was filled with those deniers.

From thenceforth, angels, those who earlier
had fulfilled god's favor, held the heaven-
kingdom's heights. The others, those fiends
who earlier had such great strife with the

wielder, lay in fire. They suffer pain, the
hot welling deep amidst hell...

.vii. . Satan's Name and Sorrow

◎ ◎ fire-brands and broad flame, as also
◎ bitter smoke, smog, and darkness. They
did not will to hold worthy the all-wielder's
words. They had much pain when they had
fallen through the fire to the bottom in that
hot hell, through mindlessness and through
over-meeting that was lacking light and full
of flame; a mighty fire's ferry.

   The fiends realized that they had wound
into uncounted pain, through their excessive
mood and through God's might and through
over-meting most of all.

   Then spoke the overly-moody king, who
earlier was the shiniest of angels, the
whitest in heaven, and his master's beloved,
dear to the chieftain until they become as
dolts in whom, for lustfulness, god himself

became mighty irked in mood. He threw
him into that murder, into that nether
curse-bed, and then shaped him a name.

The highest one said he should be
called Satan from now on, and ordered
him to care for hell's dark ground, not
at all winning against god!

Satan proclaimed; he who should
hold hell henceforth, caring for that
ground, spoke sorrowfully. Earlier, he
was god's angel, white in heaven, until
his mind forsook him, and his over-
meting most of all, because he would
not hold worthy the riders' chieftain's
words. His mind welled up in him, and
about his heart; heat was outside him,
wrathful pain.

Then he spoke with words: "This
lonely homestead is quite unlike that

other home, that one which we knew before, high in the heaven-reach*, that one which my master loaned me, though, because of the all wielder, we could not own it, make our reach roomier. But he has not done right when he has made us fall into fire at the bottom, that hot hell. He took the heaven-reach. He has marked it for mankind as a settlement. That is the most sorrow for me: that Adam, who is wrought of earth, shall hold my strong seat!

"It will be for him in joy, and we endure pain? Harm in this hell? Ah! The woe! If I could wield ownership over my hands, might become out for one time, be for one winter... then I... with this army! But iron bonds lay on me! Rope fetters ride me! I am reach-less! Hard hell-clamps have caught me fast!

* Word choice suggested by Leonardo Valdes, Cuban poet

"Here is much fire, over and nether. I have never seen a more loathsome landscape. The flame will not wane, hot over hell. A coil of rings, a cruel hard rope, has marred me from my treks, has ferried me from my path. My feet are bound, my hands are fettered. These hell-doors'ways are forfeit, so I may not a whit from these trek-bonds. Great grids of hard, heat-forged irons lay around me. With these, god has tied me by the neck, so I know he reads my mind.

"And he, the riders' cheiftain, also knows this: that it should become evil between us two, Adam and me, about the heavenly-reach, if I wield ownership of my hands.

.viii. The Fiend's Grim Array

But now, we endure new torments in hell. They are dark and hot, grim, groundless. God himself has swept us into dark mists, though he may not charge us with any sin that we carried out, loath-some to that land, even though he has shown us from the light, wrapped us in the most pain of all. We may not carry out wreck for this, repay him a whit of loathing, because he has shown us from the light.

"Now he has marked a middle-earth, where he has wrought man after his one likeness, with whom, after, he will set in heavens' reach with clear souls.

"We should yearningly consider this: that we, if we ever may, might best our anger on Adam and his heirs as

well, though winding his will to sin
if we may think it a whit. Now, for
me, I do not hope further for that light
which he thinks about long enjoying
with them, those riches with his angels'
craft. We may not win that in oldness,
because we might weaken god's mighty
mood.

  "Now, let's wind the heaven-reach
away from men's sons, now that we
may not have it, make it that they
forsake his favor, that they wind away
from men's sons, now that we may
not have it, make it that they forsake
his favor, that they wind away from
what he bids with words. Then he
will become in a wrathful mood with
them, drive them away from his favor.
Then they shall seek this hell and these

grim grounds! Then we may have them for ourselves as younglings, human sons in these fast clamps.

"Now, let's begin to think about the trek. If though the years I ever gave any thane princely treasures, when we sat luckily in that good reach and wielded our own seats, then he could not repay me for my gift with a loan at a more lovely time. If yet a young one – which of my thanes! – becomes an ally, so that he might come up hence and out through the cluster, and had craft with him so that he might fly with a feather-cloak winding through clouds.

"There Adam and Eve stand, wrought in the earth-reach; the reach by right. The rule is bestowed upon mankind. That is so sorrowful to me in my mood, it vexes me in my mind, that they will own the heaven-reach until the oldest age.

"If any of you may wind it a whit that they forsake God's lore, his word, they will soon be more loathsome to him. If they break his bidding, then he will become enraged with them; after that, the good will wind away from them and pain will be made ready for them, some hard harmful torment.

"Dream up, you all, how you might swindle them out of this! Then, I may rest more softly in these chains if they lose that reach. He who does that, a reward will be ready for him beyond old age, that which we may win henceforth down here, in this fire. I will let him sit with me myself, whosoever comes to this hot hell saying the unworth,

by word and deed,... the heaven-king's
lore.

[TWO MISSING MANUSCRIPT LEAVES]

.xi. The Fiend Temps Adam

Then god's enemy began to gear himself
up, eager in armor. He had an evil
mind. He set a sick helmet on his
head and bound it very hard,
pinned it with clasps. He knew for himself
many a speech of whirling words.

Thence, he wound himself upward,
wrenched himself through the hell-door.
He had a strong mind. He lept into the air,
his being loathsomely wrapped, and sliced
the fire in two by a fiend's craft. He
willed to delude the chieftain's younglings
secretly, with sinful deeds, to mislead
and misteach, so they would become
loathsome to god.

Then he ferried himself through
fiend's craft until he readily found

Adam, god's wisely-wrought hand-craft,
and his wife, the fairest lady, together.
As they knew too much good already, mankind's
meter himself marked them as his younglings.
And they stood between two beams that were
laden on the outside with produce, clothed
with fruit, as god the wielder, the high
heaven-king, had set with his hands,
so that these men's children might make
a choice: good or evil, each person,
wellness or woe.

   The fruit was not alike!

   One was joyful, light and shiny,
lithe and lovely; that was life's beam.
Able to live ever after, being in the world,
he who bit that fruit, so that ever after,
oldness would not hurt him, more severe
sickness, but he could always be straightaway

in desire and own his life, the heaven-king's favor, here in this world. He could have known rank to become in the high heaven, when he would hence.

The other was black all over, dim and shadowed; that was death's beam. It bore much bitterness. Both should know, in any age, that evil and good wind through this world. They should henceforth live in pain with sweat and sorrow. So be it for whomever has tasted what grows on that beam! Age shall take honorable deeds, dreams, and lordships from him, and death shall be shared with him. For a while he shall enjoy his life then, seeking the darkest of lands in the fire, where there is the most fear of all his people, he shall serve fiends for a longer while.

The loathsome one, the devil's dire go-between who fought with the chieftain, readily knew that. Then he warped himself into a worm's likeness and wound himself about

that death's beam though devil's craft, took
some fruit from there and wound away thence
to where he knew the king's handiwork to
be.

Then, the loathsome one began to ask him
with lies from the first words: "Do you long
a whit, Adam, up to god? I am faring
hither from afar on this errand. It is now
not long since I was seated with him myself.
Then he commanded me to fare on this trip;
he commanded that you eat of this produce,
said that your ability and craft and
your mood-safe would become more, and
your body much more light, your shape
much more shiny. It said that you would
not lack any thing in the world.

"Now, you have to will the heaven king's
wrought favor and serve your master
with thanks. You have wrought yourself
dear with the chieftain. In his light, I

I have heard him love your deed and
word and speak about your life. So
you shall track what his go-betweens bring
hither to this land. The green yards are
wide in the world, and god, the all-wielder
above, sits in the highest heavens' reach. He
does not wish to have this labor for himself:
that he, the human's chieftain, fare on this
trek; but he sent his youngling to speak
to you.

"Now, he has commanded me to teach
you skills with a story. Eagerly follow
his message. Take this fruit in hand. Bite it
and taste. You will become roomy in breast,
lighter in your form. God the wielder has
sent you from this help from the heaven-reach."

Adam proclaimed from where he stood on
earth, a self-shaped man: "When I heard
the victory chieftain, mighty god, proclaim
with a strong voice, and he ordered me
to stand here, to hold his bidding, and

gave me this bride, a light-shiny wife, and he ordered me to beware that I not become deluded in this death's beam, to be seduced greatly. He said that the black hell should hold he who loathsomely led a whit from his heart. I don't know, though, if you fare with lies though secret thought, or if you are the chieftain's go-between from heaven.

"Listen I cannot know your pattern a whit, words or ways, treks or sayings. I know that what he bid me himself, our savior, when I saw him last. He ordered me to hold worthy his words and hold them well, track his lore. You be not like any of his angels which I have seen before, nor have you shown me any token that he, my master, might send to me though his favor. For this, I cannot hear you, but you may go forth. I have fast belief up to the almighty god who wrought me here with his own arms and with his own hands. He may give me every good from his high reach, tho he need not send his youngling."

XII. The Worm Deceives Eve

Wrathful in mood, he wound to where he saw the wife, Eve, standing on the earth-reach, her shape shining. He said that, as for their heirs ever since, the most of harms would come in the world. "I know god the wielder will be enraged with you two as I myself am telling this outcome to him myself, when I come from this trek over a long way, as I am saying that you did not well track such an errand which he thus sends hither on this trek from the east. Now, he shall fare himself with his answer to you two. His errand-boy may not announce his message. For this,

I know that he, mighty in mood, will become enraged with you two.

"If you, willing wife, will hear my words, you may think of a roomy solution for this. Be mindful in your breast that you two both may ward off pain, as I advise. Eat of this fruit! Then your eyes will become so light that you may afterwards see so widely over all the world, and your master's own seat, and have his favor henceforth.

"Afterwards, you may stir Adam, if you have his will and he trusts your words if you say to him in truth that which you have yourself as an example in your breast. Since you abide by the tracks of god's lore, he will answer this loathsome strife, this evil, and forgo it in

his breast's coffers, if we both speak to him
with skill. Spur him on eagerly that he
tracks your lore, lest you two yet by
need become loathsome to god, your wielder.

"If you make that attempt, you the best
of ladies, I will hide from your master that
Adam spoke so much harm to me with
the weakest of words. He mistrusts me for
treachery, says I am eager for trouble,
a message-sayer of the grim, not at all
god's angel. But I know all so well the
angel's order, the high heaven's lids.

"The while was this long that I eagerly
served God, through a fixed mind, my master,
the chieftain himself. I am not like a devil!"

He led her with such lies and spurred
her on with skill, the lady into the
un-right, until the worm's thought began
welling inside her (the meter had marked

her mind weaker) that she let her mood
follow that lore. Therefore, over the chieftain's
word, at that loathsome moment, she took
the grievous fruit from death's beam.

No worse deed has ever marked mankind!

It is much wonder that eternal god, the
prince, would afterward endure that so
many a thane would be misled by those
lies which came before that lore.

She ate of that fruit! She broke the
all-wielder's word and will!

Then, she could see widely through the
loathsome one's loan, he who deceived her
with lies, seduced in secret, who came
to her for his evil deeds, so that she
thought heaven and earth whiter, and all
the world lighter, and god's work much
and mighty, though she did not see it
through human thought. Rather, the scathing

one eagerly stepped in about the soul where he
loaned her the sight so that she might gaze
so widely over heaven's reach.

Then the hateful one spoke, though
friendship. He learned her nothing good. "Now
you may see yourself, so I have no need to say
to you, Eve the good, that fruit and light are
unalike, since you trusted my words, listened
to my lore. Now the light shines before you,
rising gladly, which I brought from god, a
bit of heaven.

"Now you may grasp it.

"Say to Adam what you have with sight
though my craft's coming. If yet, through
chaste habit, he listens to my lore, then
I will give him enough of that light,
that in which I have guided you so
goodly.

"I will not punish him for his dark

sayings, though he is not worthy to be left off;
he spoke many a loathsome thing to me."

So ever after heirs shall live: when they
do loathsome things, they shall work lovingly
to better the harmful speech against the master
and have his favor thenceforth.

Then, the shiniest of ladies walked to
adam, the lightest of wives who have come
into the world because he was heaven-
king's hand-work, though she had become
secretely undone, mislead with lies, so
that they should become loath to god
through that wrathful thought, led to
doom through the devil's plot, to lack
the heaven reach's master's favor for many
a while

He is full of woe, the man who does
not check himself when he has the
power to wield himself!

One she bore in her hand, the other lay
at her heart, the apple of unblessing, which
earlier the chieftains' chieftain forbade her,
the death beam's fruit, and about which
wonder's lord spoke words that men, his
thanes, had no need to suffer the great
death. But he, holy chieftain, had given
each person the heaven-reach, wide-broad
wealth, if they would let that one fruit
be, that which the loathsome tree bore
on its beam, filled with bitterness.
That was death's beam, which the chieftain
forbid.

He misled her with lies, he who was
loath to god, in the heaven-king's hatred,
and Eve's mind, the wife's weak thought,
so that she began to trust his words, to
learn from his lore, and taken the belief

that he had brought those behests from god, those which he said to them with such oath-words, revealed a token to her and promised her his trust, his steady favor.

Then, she spoke to her master: "Adam, my lord, this fruit is so sweet, blissful in the breast, and the message-bearer, god's good angel, is shining. I see by his gear that he is our master's, the heaven-king's errand sayer. It is better for us to win his favor than his withering meting.

"If this day you spoke to him a whit of harm, he yet forgives it if we two will listen to him as younglings.

"For what should you loathsomely

strive with your master's message bearer?
His favor is needed for us two. He may deliver
an errand to the all wielder for us, to the
heaven king. I may see from here where he
himself sits (that is south and east) wound
in goodness, he who shaped the world. I
see his angels hovering around him with
feather-cloaks, the foremost of all folk, the
most joyful of riders.

"Who might give me such wits if god,
heaven's wielder, did not send it directly?

"I may hear roomily and so wide,
across the whole world over this broad
creation! I may hear sky games in heaven!
It became for me light in mind, outside
and inside, since I bit of that fruit!

"Now I have it here in my hand, my
master the good. It gives you it eagerly.
I believe that it comes from god, brought

by his behest, as his message-bearer said
to me with oath-words. It is not a whid
like all on earth, but as this honorable
one says, it comes directly from god."

.xiii. Adam's Sorrow.

He spoke to him, laid it on thick, and
spurred him on all day to that dim
deed, that they break their chieftain's
will. That wrathful message bearer stood,
laid lusts upon them, and spurred them
with skills, set them forward fiercely. The fiend
was fully near, he who had fared on that fierce
campaign over a long way; he minded the people,
to warp men into that great death, mislearning
and misleading, so they would forgo god's
loan, the almighty's gift, the heaven reach's
wielding.

Listen: the hell-scather readily knew
that they should have god's ire and hell-
binding, find by need the narrow curse,

since they had broken apart god's
bidding when he mislearned the shining
lady, the highest of wives, lying words
to them, ill advice, so that she spoke
his will, was a help to him in unlearning
god's handiwork.

Then she, shiniest of ladies, spoke to
Adam, laid it on thickly, until the thane
began to warp his mind so that he trusted
that order which the wife said with words.
She did it, though, with a fixed mind, not
knowing that so many harms, sinful
campaigns, should follow for mankind,
because she took into her mood what she
heard in the loathsome messenger's
lore, but she thought that she wrote
the heaven king's favor with those
words, because she offered the man such
tokens and orders truly until within

Adam's breast his mind twisted and his heart began to wind her will. From the wife, he grabbed hell and a trek hence, though it was not so called but it should own the name fruit. Nevertheless, it was death's dream and the devil's bond, hell and a trek hence and the holies' forlorning, humanities' murder, which they made into meat, unfaithful fruit.

As it came inside him, a horn at his heart, then the bitter-minded message bearer laughed and played, said thanks to his master for two things: "Now, I have knowingly wrought your favor for myself, and carried out your will for full many a day. Men are mislead: Adam and Eve! The wielder's disfavor for them is known, now that they have forgone word-craft, his lore. Therefore, they may no longer hold the heaven-reach, but they shall to hell on the dark trek.

"So you have no need to bear sorrow about it in your breast, where you lie bound, mournful in mood, so that men may occupy the high heaven here, though we two now suffer harms and threatening work, and shadow-land. And through your mighty being, we have forgone many things in the heaven-reach: high timbers and goodly yards.

"God became irate with us two because we two kneel with heads in the heaven-reach before the holy chieftain as younglings, but it was not yearning for us that we two willed to serve him in thane-ship. Therefore the wielder became wrathful in mood at us, hard in heart, and drove us into hell, into that fire-field the best of folks, and with his hands afterwards made the sky seats right and gave that reach to mankind.

"May your mood be blissful in your breast, because here two things are done: both that the holies' children shall forgo the heaven-reach for people and, in vengeance for that twist toward you in hot flame, I also made harm—a sorrowful mood—for god!

"So, whatever of murder we suffer here, it is now all repaid upon Adam with the master's hate and with the holies' forlornment, in men with murder's death.

"Therefore, my mood is healed, my mind is made roomy about my heart, all of our harms are wrecked for the loathing that we two long suffered. Now I will be too near the flame ever after. I will seek Satan there. He is in the dark hell, held with rings of chains."

He turned himself back nether, bitterest of message-bearers. He should seek broad flames, hell's hills, where his master lay, sealed with flames.

Both of these two sorrowed, Adam and Eve. And between them mournful words often went. They dreaded god's, their master's, hate; they were quite unsettled by the heaven-king's curse. They themselves understood his unwound word. The wife grieved, her sad mood wailed (she forwent god's favor, his love) when she saw the light slip away, that token which he who advised them to loss had revealed to her in untruth, so that they should have a hell-curse, uncontrollable humiliation. Therefore, mind-sorrow burned in their breasts.

In a while, the marriage-bound fell
together in prayer, and greeted the good
victory-chieftain, and named god, heaven's
wielder, and bid him that they must have
harming scars, going along fully and
eagerly, as they had broken god's bidding
They saw their bare body-cloaks. They
had not yet established halls on the
land, nor did they know a whit about
work's sorrow. But they might have lived
well in that land if they would have
carried out god's lore before!

They spoke many of the sorrow-words
together, the marriage-bound two.

Adam made sound and spoke to
Eve: "Listen, Eve, you have marked an evil
trek for our two selves. You now see the
dark hell, greedy and giving. Now, you

may hear it, grim hence. The heaven-reach
is not like that flame, but it is the best
of lands, which we two may have had
thanks to our master if you hadn't heard
him who advised us to this harm so that
we both broke the wielder's word, the
heaven king's.

Now we both may harrowingly sorrow for
this trek, because he himself bid us both that
we should beware of our punishment, the most
of all harms. Now hunger and thirst slit
me bitterly in the breast, though we both
once were without worry for either for all
time.

"How shall we both now live or be in this
land? If the wind comes here? From west
or east? From north or south? If mist flares
up? If hail's scourge comes pressing from

heaven? If frost, which be fearfully cold, fares mingled? In a while, heat shines from heaven, the bright sun blazes, and we too stand here bare, unguarded by clothes. Not a whit is before us two for shading the scourge, nor a whit of supply marked for our meat, but mighty god, the wielder, is wrathful in mood with us.

"Whom shall we two now become?

"Now, it may pain me that I bid heaven's god, wielder the good, that he wrought you here for me, from my body, now that you have mislead me to my master's hate.

"So now it may pain me, even into old age, that I saw you with my eyes!"

.XIIII. Adam's Woe

Eve, shiniest of ladies, brightest of wives, spoke then after. She was god's work, though she had become deluded by the devil's craft. "You may hurt me for it, my friend Adam, with your words, though it may not pain you worse in mind than it does me at heart."

Then Adam answered her: "If I knew the wielder's will, what should I have from him as a harmful scar? You will never see anything more quickly! Even if heaven's god, in hate, now orders us to fare, wading in a flood, it would not be as fearfully deep as this! No ocean-streams as this! For that, my mood has become forever betrothed to his.

"But I would go into the ground if I might work god's will.

"There is no need for me in this world,
any friendship, now that I have forgone
my prince's favor, such that I may never
have it again.

"But we two may not be a whit bare,
both of us together! Let us go into this
wood, into this forest's shade."

The two both whirled, mournfully
going into the green wood; they sat
sundered. They abided the heaven-king's
shaping, his own, as they might not have
had when almighty god forgave them
before. Then they thatched their bodies with
leaves.

They wore the woods!

They had no clothing, but they fell in
begging, the two both together, each morning,
begging the mighty one, so that god almighty

would not forget them, and so that
wielder the good should show them how
to live henceforth in the light

[END OLD-SAXON SATON SECTION]

Then, over the midday, the lord almighty,
the famous prince, came walking in
paradise, of his own will. Our savior,
forgiving father, willed to find out what
his chieftain had done. He knew the
un-made, those to whom he had before
given life.

Then they left to go from him, sad
at heart, under tree shade, bereft of
glory. They hid themselves in shadows
when they heard the chieftain's holy
word.

And they feared him!

Then the sky's lord began to call.

the created world's ward; the powerful prince ordered his son to go rapidly toward him. Then he answered him, proclaimed in humiliation the need of clothing: "My life-lord, I hide myself here, lacking clothes; I thatch myself with leaves. My shame sores me, a wretch, a scar on my spirit. Now, I dare not come forth before you, in your presence. I am all, all naked!"

.xv. The Worm Punished

Readily then god answered him: "Say this to me, my son: for what do you shamefully seek the shade? You felt no shame at me before, but you in all things! Why do you know woe and cover shame? Why do you see sorrow

and thatch yourself, your body with
leaves? Why do you speak with life-
care, lowly, mind-gloomy, such that
you are in need of clothing, unless you
ate an apple from that wood-beam which
I forbade you with words?"

Then after, Adam answered him:
"My lord chieftain, my bride, this free-
woman, gave me the fruit in the hands,
which I took as an insult to you. Now
I bear this token, a sign on myself. I
know sorrow the more!"

Then almighty god asked Eve about
this: "What have you done, ample
fellowship's, new creation's, paradise's,
growing gift's daughter, when you,
coveting, gripped onto a beam, took

the fruit on the tree's branch and, in defiance of me, ate that no good thing? You gave Adam the fruits which were fastly forbidden to you both by my words!"

Then the free-willed kinswoman, the lady ashamed in mood, answered him: "The adder, the stained worm, betrayed me, and zealously pushed me through fair words to the misshaped deed and guilty craving until I basely carried out the fiend's order. I wrought enmity and then I ravished the beam in the grove, as was not right, and then I ate the fruit."

Then our savior, lord almighty,

shaped wide treks for the adder, the
stained worm, and spoke these words.
"You, cursed one, shall widely forever
tread the earth on your breast, your
belly, going footless as long as life
dwells in you, a ghost within. You
shall eat grit for your life-days
since you loathsomely originate crime.
That wife will despise you, she will
hate you under the heavens and will
tread on your head, stained one, with
her foot. You shall await her heel,
a new battle. Between your offspring
will be cursed strife for you both
as long as the world stands under
the clouds.

"Now you will know and feel the scathing, people's loathing! How shall you live!"

.XVi. Abel's Tree

Irate, god then spoke to Eve: Wind yourself from joy! You shall be in the weaponed-man's wielding, with fear of the warrior, firmly narrowed, suffering humiliation for your deed's error, abiding death and giving birth in the world through weeping and regret, sons and daughters though much sorrow."

The eternal chieftain, life's light-bringer, also bid Adam a loathsome errand:

"You shall seek another homeland, a joyless dwelling, and you, paradise's naked clothes needer, turn in wreck, dealt from goods. For you, body and soul have become dealt.

Listen! Now we will hear where harmful things and world-pain awoke for us.

Wonder's guardian guided them with clothes. Our shaper ordered them to thatch their shame with the first rags. He ordered them to wind from paradise into a narrower life

By the lord's behest, the holy angel locked pleasures' and joys' hopeful home in their tracks with a fiery sword. No crafty one, not any sin-guilty man, may pass though. But the guard has might and strength; he holds that shining life for the fellowship dear unto the chieftain.

However, the almighty, the founding father, did not will to take all from Adam and Eve, though he might have wound from them. But, as a comfort for them from thence forth, he let the high-standing roof be with holy stars and gave them ample ground-wealth. He ordered each of the sea's and the earth's offspring bearing species to feed the married couple fruits, according to worldly need.

They settled after sin in a more sorrowful land, earth and homeland more unyielding in every benefit than the first seat was, that which they were driven from after the deed.

Then they began, by God's behest, to beget children, as the meter bid them. Adam's and Eve's heirs were born, two free-willed first-sons, Cain and Abel.

The books make known to us, dear brothers, how these first-doers amassed goods, wealth, and food. One tilled his glory from the earth. He was born earlier. The other held cattle as a help to his father until a great many of counted days went forth. Then they both brought the chieftain an offering. The angels' prince saw Abel's yield with his eyes.

All creatures' king willed not to see Cain's offering. For that man, pain was heavy upon the heart. Mind-stress arose, blatant strife in the man's breast, ire because of envy. He then carried out an unarrayed act with his hands; he slew his free-kinsmen, his own brother, and spilt his blood, Cain of Abel.

Middle-earth swallowed that one's death-gore, man's blood, after the slaughter-stroke. Woe, pain's progeny, was reared. Ever since, from that twig horrible fruits have loathsomely grown, longer and more strongly. That crime's boughs have spread widely throughout men's homelands

ABEL'S
TREE

Frida Portugal

2L, May 2018

The harmful branches, severely and sorely,
have struck mankind's sons.

They still do!

From them, broad blades of every
evil began to sprout!

We must lament that story,
slaughter-grim wyrd, with weeping,
not at all without cause. Why did
the free-willed woman severely harm
us through first sin, since Adam
became quickened with a ghost
from god's mouth.

.xvii. Cain's Curse and Offspring

Wonder's elder then asked
with a word where on earth
Abel might be.

Then the worthless one,
murder's craftsman, quickly

answered after that. "I do not know
abel's coming or going, my dear
kinsmen's trek. Nor was I my brother's
herdsman."

Then, the angels' prince, the good
power ghost, made speech again: "Why
did you make the oath-fast warrior
fall, your own sibling with your
wrathful hand, your brother? And
why does his blood cry out and
call to me? For that murder, you
shall win pain and roam in
wreck, accursed for your wide life.
The earth will not lightly give
you fruits for worldly need, but
she has previously swallowed the
slaughter-gore from your hands.

Therefore, she will deprive you of splendor; the green fold will deprive you of brightness. You shall roam gloomily, lacking honor from earth as you became Abel's life-bane. Therefore, you shall wander the wide track as a fleer, loathsome to dear kinsmen."

Then Cain answered him: "I need not expect any honor in the world-kingdom because I have forfeit heavens' high king, your favor, love and peace. Therefore, I shall lay tracks, widely, awaiting woe. Whenever one meets the sin-evil me, far or near, he may remind me of that crime, of brother-killing. I shed his blood, gore onto

the earth. You, on this day, condemn me
from joys and drive me from my earth.
Some wrathful one will become my life-
bane. I, accursed, shall wander from
your sight, Prince."

Then, victories' chieftain himself
replied: "Now, you need not dread
death's terror, life-killing, yet, though
you shall go on a trek, marked, away
from free-kinsmen. If any man slays
your life with his hands, sevenfold
vengeance will come upon him after
that sin, pain after works."

Upon him, the wielder, the glory-fast
meter, the lord, set a token, a
protection-beacon upon him, lest any
fiend dare greet him with witchcraft,
from far or near. She he ordered the

sin-guilty one to wind away from
mother and kinsmen, his family.
Then Cain went from him, going gloomy-
mooded from the good sight, a friend-
less wretch. And then he chose for
himself a dwelling in the eastern
lands, a native place far from his
father-yard. There, a free-willed
kinswoman, a lady after nobility, fed
heirs for him. The first was called Enos,
Cain's first born.

    Afterward, he began to build a
fortified city with his kinsmen. This
was the first of all fortified walls
under the clouds, that which the
sword-bearing princes ordered to be
set. Thence, his heirs first awoke,

born from the bride in that homestead.
The first was called Jared, Enos's son.
Afterwards awoke those who enlarged
that kind's family size, Cain's lineage.
Malalehel was after Jared, a cattle-herd
in his father's tracks until he went
forth. Afterwards, Mathusal dealt
princes' treasure to his kinsmen for
birth after birth, amongst his brethren,
until the elder's departure carried
him away, old in long days, letting
off his life. Lameh received the family
treasures, the household goods, after his
father's day. For him, two brides, ladies
in the native land, Ada and Sella,
feed heirs.

One's name was Jabal, Lamech's
son, he who first though glowing
thought awoke the harp's sound
from his hands amongst those
dwelling here first, the sweet victory
song.

.xviii. Cain's Death and Seth's Offspring.

Likewise, in the tribe at the same
time, there was a kinsmen called
Tubalcain. He, though smith-
craft's wisdom-power and and
though thoughtful mood was man's
first plow-worker; he was first over
the field. Afterwards, those born of the
folk knew bronze and iron, city dwellers
enjoying widely.

Then, Lamech himself said words to

his two wives, beloved bedmates, Adan
and Sellan, an honorless story: "I slew
in murder one of my favored kinsmen.
I stained my hands in Cain's killing;
with my hands, I felled Enos's father,
Abel's spear-bane. I sealed his
slaughter-gore in earth. I know
readily what comes in that bodily
death's tracks. The true kind's
sevenfold wreck, mighty after a sinner.
My fall, my soul-killing; I shall
quickly be guided with a grim guide.
This I know."

Meanwhile, in payment for Abel, another
heir in the native land was born for
Adam, a truth-fast son. His name was
Seth. He was blessed, and freely, as a

comfort, he enlarged his elders, father
and mother, Adam and Eve. It was Abel's
yield in the worldly-reach. Then
mankind's origin spoke a word:
"Victories' wielder has eternally sealed
a son for me, myself — life's elder.
for the beloved stolen, he who Cain
slew. — and our prince has shoved
the sad sorrow away from my mood
with his kinship-branch. Thanks to
him for this!"

    Adam had — when he began begging
others for himself as native heirs, births
by his bride, born noble — thirty and
a hundred of this life's winters in
the world. The writings say to us that
here, for eight hundred afterwards, he grew
in kin-size with men and maidens.

Adam had nine-hundred winters, and thirty also, in all on earth when he had to give up this world though his ghost's departing.

Beloved Seth rode in his tracks. Heir after elder, he held the native seat and got himself a wife. He had five and a hundred winters when he first began to grow his kin-group, his men, with sons and daughters. His heir, his seed's eldest, was called Enos. He named god. None of all those born first since Adam saw greener grass. A worthy ghost! Seth was blessed! Afterwards for eight hundred and seven years here, he begot sons and daughters. He had twelve and nine-hundred when the time came that he should take peaceful parting.

Enos held after Seth, when he went from the world, with Enos as heir since the earth swallowed up seed-bearing Seth's body. He was well-loved and lived here a hundred ninety winters before he brought forth births here by his wife though bed-sharing. Then Cainan was born to him first, an heir in the native land. During eight-hundred in the Chieftain's protection, the glowing-souled hero begot youths, sons and daughters. He died when he had five and nine-hundred, that wise old man.

Then after Enos, Cainen was the kin-group's elder-doomer, guard and wise-one. He had just seventy winters before a son awoke for him. Then

the heir was fed in the homeland.
Cainen's son was called Malalehel.
During eight-hundred winters, and
forty also, he increased the princes'
number by souls. Enos's son had
nine-hundred winters, and five also,
in all when he gave up this world.
Then his tiding of days under the
roomy sky was filled in number.

.XViiii. Enox and Noe

In his tracks, Malalehel held the land
and goods for a swarm of seasons.
The first-spear had five and
sixty winters when he began begetting
children by a wife. The bride brought
him a son, a maiden into mankind.
He was powerful in his tribe, they tell me,
a warrior from youth called Jared,

Malalehel, afterwards, lived here long
and enjoyed bliss, mankind's dream,
here among worldly-treasures. He had
five and ninety winters, and eight-
hundred, when he went forth. He left
heirs, land, and tribal guardianship.
Long since, he brought guys gold
gear. The earl was noble, an honor-
fast hero, and the first-spear was
beloved to his free-kinsmen.

   He, Jared, lived in this life five
hundred, and sixty also, abided
winters in the worldly-reach when
the time came that his wife brought
a son into the world. That heir was
called Enoc, freely first-born. Then
yet from here the father grew his

kin's family size, his heirs, through
eight hundred years. He had five and
sixty, and nine-hundred also, years in
all, reckoned by nights, when he went
forth, winter's old friend when he
gave off this world and then glowingly
left the land and tribal-yard ready,
beloved warrior.

Afterward, Enoch heaved up the lead-
deeming, the folk's wise protective power.
He would not at all let his dominion and
chieftainship fall! While he was the head-
kinsmen's herder, he enjoyed happy days,
begot births, for three hundred winters. The
tribal elder, heaven's wielder, was held
to him. Henceforth, the warrior sought
bliss in his body the chieftain's power.
He did not suffer the middle-yard's death

at all, as men do here, young and old,
when from them god takes away owned
things and earthly treasure's presence
and their leadership also.

But he went quickened.

He fared away from this loaned
life with the angel's king, in the gear
which his ghost wore before a mother
brought him to mankind. He left the
folk to the eldest heir, the first-born.
He had five and sixty winters, and
also three hundred, when he gave off
this world.

For a time after, Mathusal held the
kinfolk's goods. He enjoyed worldly dreams
in a body the longest. He begot many
sons and daughters before his death-day.
The wise old holy one had nine-hundred
winters, and seventy two, when he should

turn from strife.

The son, Lamech, after him, held the tribal guardianship. For long since, he enjoyed the world. He had two and a hundred winters when it became time that the earl began to beget noble ones, sons and daughters. Since then, he lived five and ninety years. The lord enjoyed many a winter under the clouds. The rider's ruler held the folk well for five hundred years more, begetting births. Descendents awoke from him, heirs and ladies.

He named the eldest Noe. Before the curse, he enjoyed the land since Lamech went. The wise-old prince had five-hundred winters when he went forth, begetting births, as the book says.

Noe's sons: the eldest was called Sem;
the other, Cham; the third, Iafeth. The
tribe grew more roomily under the skies;
the number of men in the kin-group
around middle-earth, sons and
daughters. And that was Seth's kin,
the beloved first tribe, bathed in the
chieftain's love and doom-ready...

.xx. Noe's Sea-House
 ⊙ until those born of god began to
⊙ ⊙ seek brides from within Cain's kin,
the cursed folk. And there, over the
meter's behest, they, men's heirs, procured
wives, sinful maidens, shiny and fair.
    Then the sky's ruler refreshed wrath
for mankind and spoke these words:
"They are not free from leaving me in

my mind, Cain's kin, but that kind has
angered me sorely! Now, those born of Seth
renew the tear and take for themselves
maidens as mates, of my fiends! Their
wives light, the ladies' appearance, pierced
fiercely, and the eternal fiend pierced
many chiefly folk who were in peace
before."

 After a hundred and twenty winters
in the world, tallied by numbers, wreck
beset the fated people when the lord
willed to set pain on the oath-breakers,
and slay to death those sinful in
deeds, giant-kin unloved by god,
mighty evil-doers loathsome to the
meter. Then victory's wielder himself
saw what men's evil was on Earth;
and they were proud of sins, full
of false wit. He unfairly thought to

wreck mankind's family, ripping through
mankind, grimly and sorely, with hard
might.

It rubbed him raw verily that he
had awoken the folk's first maiden,
princes' origin, when he shaped Adam.

He said that for men's sins he would
lay waste to all that was on earth,
forlorning each of the bodies which
thatched the life's ghost within. The
lord would have killed all, in the
approaching tide, in that which
nauled those born of the curse.

Noe was good, beloved to the
savior, greatly blessed, Lamech's
son, doom-fast and meek. The
chieftain knew that the prince's

zeal firmed the thoughts in his
breast. Therefore, the king said
to him, holy in voice, all-creature's
helmet, what curse he willed to

carry out against men. He saw
the earth, filled with the un-right,
wide rich fields laiden with sins,
marked with stains.

The wielder spoke, our savior,
and said to Noe: "I will kill all
the folk with a flood, and every kind
of quick creature, those which the
lofty sky and flood lead and feed,
beasts and birds. You shall have
peaceful shelter with your sons when
dark water, wan slaughter-streams,

swallows the riders, the sinful scathers. Begin to work yourself a ship, a great sea-house. In that, you shall provide rest and right seats for the many offspring of earth, each after his own. Shape shelves in the ship's bosom. There, you will work a ferry fifty-wide, thirty high, thirty long, measured by els, and work the fixtures fast against the waves. There shall be each quick-living kind's offspring in that wooden fortress, fruit of earth's offspring led. The ark shall be the more!"

Noe did as his savior ordered,

heard the holy heaven-king, and began
at once to work that temple, the mighty
sea-chest. He said to his kinsmen that
a dreadful thing came toward the people,
the wrathful punishment. They did not
heed that. Then, after a swarm of
winters passed, the oath-fast meter
saw the best of sea-houses, Noe's
ferry, towering, geared, made fast against
the flood inside and out with choice earth
lime.

    That singular kind! It will be even
the harder when rough water, dark streams,
beats it more strongly.

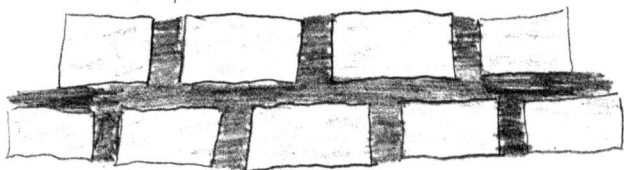

.xxi. The Rider's Chieftain Wields the Waters

O ur Savior then spoke to Noe: "I present you this, most beloved of men, my oath: that you will take to the waves, along with life's offspring, which you shall ferry around the deep water, enduring a number of days, in the ship's bosom. Lead, as I order you, your heirs under the ark-boards, the three first spears and your four wives.

"And you will take onto that sound-hall seven, tallied by number, of each offspring, those which gave life to men as meat, and two of all the others. Likewise, you will load, wise under the wave-board, fruits from all the earth for the riders, those who shall survive

the sea-flood with you. Freely feed life's
awoken until I will to craft order under
the sky again for the lake-treker's leaving

"Now, you will withdraw with your
household, going into the temple, ghosts'
riders. I know you well, fast-minded one.
You are worthy of peaceful shelter, honor
with your heirs. I will now over seven
nights let slaying rain fall over the
wide earth's face. For forty days, I will
strike vengeance on warriors, and with
a wave-throng, kill all, owned and
owner, whatever may be outside the
ark-boards when the dark storm begins
stirring"

Then Noe himself went, as his savior

ordered, under the ark-boards, leading heirs,
men and their wives together on the wave-
plank, and all the lord almighty willed
to have as seed flared under the roof to
their food-giver, just as the almighty, the
rider's chieftain, bid them through his
words. The heavenly reach's guard locked
the sea-house's mouth upon their heals with
his own hands, victories' wielder, and
signed the ark inside by his own ability
our savior.

Noe, Lamech's son, had six hundred
winters when he climbed under boards
with his sons, glowing amongst younglings,
by god's behest, dear fellows.

The chieftain sent rain from the skies,

and also widely let well-springs surge
upon the world. Black terror-streams
swelled from every well. Seas surged up
over shore-walls. He was strong and
wrathful, he who wielded the waters.
He wreathed and swallowed those born
of middle-earth's man-feud, men's
native land with wan waves. He
harried temples. The meter wreaked mind
torments upon men. The sea strongly grip-
ped the hateful folk for forty days, and
nights as well. Ruin was rampant, a
grim-slaying for men. The wonder-king's
waves wrenched the honorless ones' lives
from their flesh-homes. The flood, raging
under the heavens, wreathed all: high
mountains, around the wide ground. And

on the sound, the flood heaved up the
ark from the earth and the nobles with
it, those who the chieftain himself, our
shaper, signed when he locked that ship.

Then over the wave's ridge under
the clouds on the wide road, the best
temple fared with cargo. The water's
violent terror was unable to touch the
wave-riders in the ferry because holy
god ferried and saved them. The flood-
drenched sea stood fifteen of man's ells,
deep over the dunes.

That was famous wyrd!

Standing here was nothing to deal
them apart, except what was heaved
up on this high loft. Then the wet-
army killed all earth's offspring but

what heaven's lord himself held in ark-
boards when holy god himself, the eternal,
let those with easy moods rise up on the
streams; stiff-minded king.

.XXii. The Raven and the Culver

Victories' wielder then minded the
sea riders, Lamech's son and all those
awoken ones that he locked against
the water, life's first light in the ship's
bosom. The rider's chieftain led the
warriors by his word over wide land.

The welling flood began to lightly lower
afterwards. The lake ebbed dark under the
sky. The true meter had already calmed
the terror stream, stilled the water; the
bright rain. The foamy ship fared for
fifty and a hundred nights under the skies
after the flood had heaved up the nailed

boards, the best ferry, until the
numbered-tally of days for the wrathful
season went forth.

Then, the best of halls, Noe's ark,
sat with cargo, high on the dunes; those
are called Armenia. The holy one, Lamech's
son, abided, awaited truthful commands
for a long time; when life's guard, lord
almighty, might give him rest from the
frightful trek. Here, he dreaded all around
when wan waves bore him widely around
the sound, beyond the traveled ground.
The sea was going

The holy riders then longed, as did
their wives, for when they might step
out of the narrow room across the nailed
board over the steam-bank and lead

possessions out of that cage. Then, the
ship's forward guard found whether the
sea-flood were yet sinking under the
clouds.

Then, as the days wore on as the high
hill harbored the hoard, and the noble
one of earth's offspring also, Lamech's
son, let a dark raven fly out
of the house over the high
flood. Noe reckoned that he—
in his need if he could not
find land over the wide water
on which to land—would seek
the wave-plank. After, the thought

left him, for the fiend perched on
a floating corpse! The dark
feathered one would not
seek!

Then, about seven nights
after he let the dark raven
fly from the ark, he let a
dusky culver fly over high
water in order to find whether
the deep, foamy sea had yet
given back any dole of the
green earth.

She widely sought her will and flew around. However, she found no rest since she could not tread upon land with feet for the flood nor step on a tree's leaf for the currents. And the steep hills were ringed with water. The wild bird went in the evening, seeking the ark, over wan waves, sinking weary and hungry, the holy warrior's hand.

Then, again, the culver was sent, after a week, from coffer to wild. She flew wildly until she,

in wild ecstasy", found a fair
resting place, and then with
feet stepped onto her beam,
blissful in mood because she
could sit, very weary, on the
tree's bright twig. She shook
her feathers, went flying away

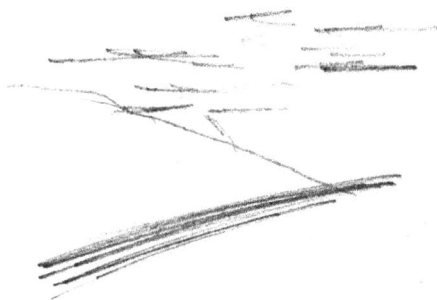

with her offering. Soaring, she
brought an oil-beam's twig to
his hand, a green blade.

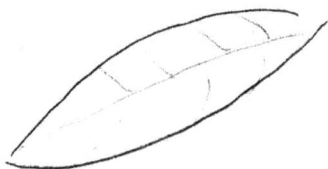

Then, the floating men's lord right
away knew that comfort had come, an end
to toilsome trek.

Then yet after a third week, the
blessed warrior sent a single wild
culver. She did not come back to the
floating boat but she claimed land,
green-groves. Afterward, the glad bird
would not show herself any more

under the pitch-dark boards within
the fastened planks when there was
no need of her

.xxiii. The Shower-Bow

ur savior then spoke to Noe, the
heavenly-reach's guardian with
holy words: "again, the native seat
is granted to you, bliss on land, rest
from lake-trek, fair in the field.
Leave, going in freedom out of the ark and
onto the earth's surface. Out of the high
temple, you shall lead your family and
all those awake I saved from the wave
threats on the slope when the lake had
thoroughly thatched it, the third homeland."

He did so and heard the lord. He
stepped over the welling-stream as the voice

bid him with much lust. And then he led
wrath's leavings over the wave-plank.

Then, fast-arrayed Noe began to ready
gifts for the savior and readily took a
dole of all his owned things, those which
the chieftain had sealed for him in
fellowship. He glowed before the yield!
And then to god himself, the bright-
mooded hero said an offering to the
angel's king. Indeed, our savior did
know the blessed Noe, and his children
also, that he had given that gift in
thanks and that earlier in youth
he had earned those gifts through
good deeds.

Then, almighty god was gracious to

him for all honors, the doom-fast fellowship
Then yet, the chieftain, wonder's elder,
said words to Noe: "Now teem and grow!
Enjoy glory with peaceful joy! Fill the
earth! Enlarge all! Yours is the native-
seat, the sea's bounty and heaven-birds
and wild beasts and fertile cattle are
sealed in your wielding on the all-
green earth!

"Never shall you eat food dishonored
with blood at your feast-table, besmitten
with sinful beast-gore.

Each of those who first grinds the
ghost from the fellowship thereby draws
out the other life with a spear-point.
He will have no need to rejoice in the

offering in thoughtful mood but I will
seek out man's life for slaying with
much swiftness and because of bloodshed
for brother-killing, strike down man's
violence with weapons, murder with hands!

"Man was first shaped to god's likeness.
Each has the meter's and the angels' aspect;
those who hold well the holy customs. Wax
and take root! Enjoy what you will!
Honor the earth! Fill all the field's corners
with noble ones from your kind, learning
and following.

'I betroth you with my seal: that I,
in middle-earth, will never again lead
a sea-army, water over wide land.

Often, gleaming in the clouds, you

will be able to see a clear token when I show my shower-bow, that I will last in my oath with men as long as the world stands!"

Then, Lamech's wise son was the treasure's herdsman; coming off the ferry, the flock in his tracks with his three heirs and their four wives. They were named Percoba, Olla, Olliva, Ollivani.

The oath-fast meter; water's leavings.

The rough-minded heroes, Noe's sons, were called Sem and Cham, the third Jafeth. From these warrior men, folk came forth. And all the middle-earth became willed with those born of men.

.XXIIII. Naked Noe

Noe then began anew, establishing a home with kinsmen and tilling the earth for eats with them. He worked and wrought, set a vineyard, saved many a seed. He yearningly sought what the light-bright fruits brought him, yearly-glowing gifts from the green field.

Then, it passed that the blessed warrior became wine-drunk in his tent. He slept a bit wearily and shoved the roof from himself, off his body, as was not fitting. He lay there limb-naked. He little got that, in his own inn, such harm dropped when head-swimming clamped onto his reason, onto his heart's holy temple. His mind-safe

went away, swiftly into sleep, so that he
could not, dropped in mind, wrap himself
in rags with his hands and thatch shame
as was shaped for a warrior and a wife
since wonder's thane locked life's native
land in the tracks behind our father
and mother with a fiery sword.

Then Cam came, trekking in first,
Noe's heir where his elder became
deprived of senses. There, he willed to
show no honor toward his aged father,
nor indeed to hide his kinsman's shame,
but he, laughing, said to his brothers how
the man himself rested within. Then, they
rather covered their faces, quickly in
wrappings, under cloaks, so they could

carry help to the beloved man. Both
were good: Sem and Iafeth.

Then, Lamech's son broke from
sleep and then soon got that Cam willed
no kin-goodness when he was bereft of
honor, willed not to know any favor or
trust. For that, the holy one was sorry in
mood. Then, he began to curse the one
born from himself with words. He said
Cam, on earth, should be humble under
the heavens, a slave to kinsmen. Then,
afterwards, he was shod terribly with
curses, and his kin-line also.

Then afterward, Noe enjoyed, along
with his sons, the reach's breadth for

three hundred winters of this life, and
fifty also; freemen after the flood. Then
he went forth. Afterwards, his heirs
enjoyed riches, amassing births. Bright
wealth was theirs.

The younglings from Iafeth became
fed, high bodied hearth-riders, sons
and daughters. He himself was kind.
He held the reach steady, the native
dreams, glory among those born to
him, until his breasts' hoard, his
glorious ghost, should go to god's
doom. Afterwards, Geomor dealt
his father's household goods to friends,
Iafeth's sons to allies and siblings.
An unlittle dole of that line's offspring

filled the shaped earth.

Likewise, Cham's sons became born,
heirs in the homeland. The eldest was
called Chus and Chanan, fully free in
spirit, Cham's first-born. Chus was head-
wise for noble-ones, a giver of willed things
and worldly fellowship for his brothers, of
family-payment in his father's tracks,
since Cham went forth from his body
when death shrouded him. The kin-
arranger said doom to his tribe until
his count of days had run out. Then,
the warrior gave up earthly goods;
Nebroth's father sought another life.

Afterwards, Chus's first-born heir
wielded the inherited seat, a widely —

famous warrior. The writing says to
us that he, in those storied days, had
the most might and strength of
mankind. He was the first of Babylon's
kingly-rulers, the original apeling. He
heaved up homeland glory, roomy and
roaring.

One common voice was still yet
among the earthbound.

.XXV. Sennar's Beacon-Tower

Likewise, from Cam's family
awoke many a warrior tribe.
Many in number of kids were
born of that wide-folk.
Then, a host of free-born sons and

daughters became fed in the worldly reach
by Sem before he, the riders' elder,
chose thence forth in the winters' slaughter-
rest. In that tribe, men were kind.
There was one called Eber, Sem's heir.
Heroes awoke from him, an uncountable
people whom princes, all the earth-
bound, now call Ebrei. They went
from the east, leading owned things,
cattle and goods.

    The folk were of one mood. Brave
warriors sought roomy land until
they became a mighty company, a
faring folk. There they born of princes
firmly took earth. Then, they set upon

Sennar, vast and wide, the tribal
arrangers in the yore-days with beloved
men. Green grasslands, fair fields were,
in those days, a forward-guard for the
fellowship, waxing the ability for each
willed thing.

Then there many a many beside his
kin-ally, princes in one mood, bid one
another that they - to grow in fame
before the men again - should ferry
born ones around the fields, tribal
kin-groups in search of land, work
a stronghold as a beacon-tower, raise
it up to the starry sky. For this,
they sought Sennar's field. Thus, the

folk's foremost arrangers, the eldest,
often and frequently dwelled with bliss.
With lore, they sought warriors to work
and for workmanship until for power
and wan minds, they made the craft
known.

They wrought a castle, and they
raised it up to heaven like a ladder.

With strength, they stepped up a
stone wall over men's measure,
yearning for fame, heroes with hands.
Then holy god came to show himself
the warrior-family's work, the born
ones' firm stronghold, and the
beacon also, that Adam's heir had

begun to rear up to the skies.

And for that ill-array, the
stiff-minded king gave pause.

Then he, wrathful in mood, set an
unlike reordering on the earth-dwellers,
such that they no longer owned power
over speech! When they, the crew at
the tower, meted out might in many
numbers, knowing the work, the
warrior tribes did not know anything
that the others said! They could not
make the stone wall come up from
the timber, but they harmfully mislaid
in heaps, dealt apart by voices. Each had
become an alien tribe to the other since

the meter, though mighty craft,
broke men's speech.

Then, those born of princes fared
away, in four ways, untribed, in
search of land. In their tracks, both
the sturdy stone tower and the steep
stronghold stood together, unwrought,
in Sennar.

Then, Sem's tribal stronghold
waxed and thrived under the clouds
until a man awoke in that family,
among a number of kin-born, a
warrior, thoughtful in mood,
mindful of customs. From that prince,
heirs became ascendant in Babylon.

The born ones were fed, the free-
bodied two. And then, the front-
spears, the high-roofed heroes, were
called Abraham and Aaron. For those
earls, the angels' lord was both
peace and life.

She, Aaron's heir became fed, beloved
in life. His name was Lop.

Then the kin-warriors, Abraham
and Lop, thrived under the meter,
unwickedly, as ~~they~~ were from old
nobility in the worldly-reach. For
this, they now deem ~~they now deem~~
those born of chieftains in fellowship.

END BOOK I
The Shaping: Satan's Saga.

Bibliography

The poem presented here was originally compiled from several sources under the reign of King Ælfræd, who ruled Anglo-Saxon England from 871-899 AD. It appears first in the 10th century in what scholars call "MS Junius 11" or simply "The Junius Manuscript." My primary source for this translation/rendering has been the digital fascimile from Oxford's Bodleian Digital Texts, edited by Bernard J. Muir, which should be consulted by anyone wishing to know more about the manuscript.

I also consulted the editions of A.N. Doane, and invite curious readers to do the same.

In preparing this translation - here the 17th draft, I used often the Bosworth-Toller Anglo-Saxon dictionary online, the Oxford English Dictionary, and the Urban Dictionary,

The Ælfrædian Foundation

The publisher pledges to use at least one dollar from each book sale to establish a charitable organization dedicated to helping teenaged victims of child abuse, particularly abuse perpetrated by Catholic priests.

Riddle #13

I was shaped by many a shaper;
I suppose my mode is mutable.
Gaze though this window at my wyrd life
I rode on the back of a beast and was free,
But a blade broke though. (I bear that scar still.)
They stripped me naked, shaved my flesh,
Then tied me up, tore me in all directions;
Every fiber of my being buckled then folded out
Time and time again, torture unbearable.
I thereafter remained rigid and enlarged.
Later, an austere artist came to me
And fixed the form you find today.
I thought my worth had withered away
Till that shaper stained me, set down words
With a wing's fallen leaf. What's my name?

www.ingramcontent.com/pod-product-compliance
Lightning Source LLC
LaVergne TN
LVHW041226080426
835508LV00011B/1093

9 780692 148907